LANZAROTE

EDICIONES A.M.

© **EDICIONES A.M.**
Telf.: 91 634 31 29
        928 81 57 61
Fax: 91 634 21 52
        928 81 57 61
Page Design: ANDRÉS MURILLO
Text: JORGE ECHENIQUE AND ANDRÉS MURILLO
Photography: ANDRÉS MURILLO AND JOSÉ BAREA
D.L.: GC. 853-2003
I.S.B.N.: 84-95822-00-8
Typesetting: VISIÓN CINCO, S.L.
Printers: SAN NICOLÁS, S.A. (Gran Canaria)

Lanzarote

On arriving in LANZAROTE the visitor feels himself transported in time, whisked back to the beginnings of the world, a fresh, clean world in which he himself is the protagonist of discovery and conquest. Here are seas of lava; enchanted grottos; columns of steam emerging from the bowels of the earth; amazing multicoloured walls of stone; enigmatic, threatening volcanos; waves that beat furiously on tortured cliffs that loom like giants frozen for all time in their march to the sea; mysterious lagoons that appear by surprise among the rocks; pockets scooped in the lava that protect the "malvasía" vines, producers of unsurpassable wine; golden beaches and transparent blue waters; a landscape from another world and another time. But this is not all in LANZAROTE, there are also people and history; a people that built peaceful, flower-bedecked white villages; the history of a people that, in overcoming the desolation caused by other men and by the fury of the earth, learned to reconstruct and to cultivate on the very lava and ashes, making use of the few drops of dew trapped by the land.

These are kind, hospitable people who offer the visitor the very best of themselves, along with the comfort of hotels, developments and sports facilities of the highest level. LANZAROTE is all this and much more, and for this reason the visitor will take with him and keep always the memory of a kaleidoscope of images and of the magic moments experienced.

Arrecife

San Ginés shoreline.

Arrecife is the commercial and administrative centre of the island, with modern buildings and colourful, shop-lined streets. But the bustle of modern life has not prevented it from conserving the character and style of the colonial fishing village it once was, as may be appreciated when strolling through the town's verdant parks or tree-lined streets of white houses, or when visiting the shoreline of the CHARCO DE SAN GINÉS, with the fishing boats hauled up onto the beach and the men repairing their nets and tackle.

Founded at the beginning of the 15th century, the peaceful fishing village of Arrecife dozed quietly for more than two hundred years until, at the beginning of the 17th century, the devastation of the then capital of the island, San Miguel de Teguise, by invading Berber pirates led the administration to transfer its activities to Arrecife, well protected by its two excellent natural harbours and defences. The castle of San Gabriel, which dominates the entire bay from the coast to the islands of EL FRANCÉS and LOS INGLESES, bears testimony to this age of adventure.

The castle of SAN GABRIEL was constructed in 1.574 by king Felipe II. In 1.586 its was razed to the ground by pirates under the orders of the privateer MORATO ARRAEZ. Legend has it that after heroic resistance by the entire town, and following the death of the menfolk, the women opted to put an end to their own lives rather than fall into the hands of the invading pirates.

Finally, in 1596, the architect LEONARDO TORRIANI reconstructed the castle, leaving it as it is today and joining it to the city by means of a bridge. This bridge, which still exists, is known as the "Puente de las Bolas" or Bridge of the Balls, because of the spherical stones topping the pillars on which it rests.

In 1779, and in order to ensure the coastal defence of the city from the north, CARLOS III built another castle between the MUELLE DE LOS MÁRMOLES and PUERTO NAOS. This castle, erected at a time when the island was stricken by labour shortage, was christened by the people as the "castillo del hambre" or castle of hunger, since those who had nothing to eat worked to build it.

Today the CASTILLO DE SAN JOSÉ houses the Contemporary Art Museum, which exhibits the works of famous modern artists.

Arrecife is still today a fishing town. Its fleet, the largest in the islands, competes with the modern, high-tech fleets of JAPAN

San Gabriel castle and Bridge of the Balls.

Museum of Contempory Art.

San José castle.

Cabildo de Lanzarote building.

Panoramic view of Arrecife and San Gabriel castle.

Reducto beach.

and RUSSIA in exploiting the Canary Bank, which stretches from LANZAROTE to the coast of the African continent.

In recent years, fishing, related industry and tourism have led to extraordinary development of the city, which is now an important commercial centre whose population amounts to half that of the entire island. The street known as LEÓN Y CASTILLO, previously CALLE REAL, is now a famous shopping area, whose establishments offer the visitor pleasant, and inexpensive, surprises.

But in spite of this economic development and the growth of its population, Arrecife has managed to maintain a spirit of harmony and balance between its offices and shops and its fishing boats and beaches.

León y Castillo street.

Costa Teguise

To the north-west of ARRECIFE is the stretch of coast known as COSTA TEGUISE, one of the island's most important concentrations of tourist installations: 5-star hotels and apartment, bungalow and chalet complexes alongside shops, restaurants, bars, pubs and a wide variety of the highest category sports facilities where the visitor may indulge in whatever individual or group sports he prefers.

This part of the coast is known as COSTA TEGUISE because a large part of it is located in the area of SAN MIGUEL DE TEGUISE, previously the capital of the island.

COSTA TEGUISE begins a few kilometres from ARRECIFE, and is dotted with coves of golden sand separated by headlands of black lava and with luxurious residential developments surrounded by a *sea of green*.

LOS MOLINOS, PLAYA BASTIAN, PUNTA DE TOPE, PLAYA DE LAS CUCHARAS, etc… are some of the most significant spots in this rosary of splendid beaches, bathed by warm crystalline waters that boast a particularly rich treasure of marine life, much appreciated by lovers of fishing, and swept by waves and wind that seem to have been created especially for those daring

Windsurfing at las Cucharas beach (Playa de las Cucharas).

Water park on the Teguise coast.

Las Cucharas beach and Meliá Salinas hotel.

Golf course." Teguise Golf Course".

Panoramic view of the beach and holiday flats.

souls whose pleasure is to ride the waters on a board driven by a sail. COSTA TEGUISE has, in fact, become famous throughout the world for the exceptional conditions it offers windsurfers, even the rawest of beginners.

The hotels, tourist centres and residential developments are first class, as regards both their quality and comfort and their especially accessible prices. Tourism to the island is continuous from one season to the next, throughout the entire year, even in Winter. Because LANZAROTE's privileged geographical location gives it a constant warm climate, tourists, especially those who come from tougher climes in search of warmth and smooth beaches accompanied by modern comforts, find on COSTA TEGUISE comfortable lodging, a wide variety of shopping centres, sports and nightlife within a frame of incomparable beauty.

Bastián beach.

Teguise

SAN MIGUEL DE TEGUISE bears the name of the beautiful daughter of GUARDAFRA, last king of the original inhabitants of the island, the "guanches", the Princess who married the knight who conquered the island for the crown of Castile, JEAN (MACIOT) de BETHENCOURT.

It was through Princess TEGUISE that the agreements and disagreements between her father, the King, and her husband, the conqueror, were channelled, and it was she who finally brought peace and understanding to reign between the two men, and their respective bands.

SAN MIGUEL DE TEGUISE, a hamlet turned city, was to become the spiritual and

Our Lady of Guadalupe church.

administrative centre of LAN7AROTE, and it was from here that the expeditions set forth to conquer the rest of the archipelago.

TEGUISE was also a meeting place between CASTILE and AMERICA during the first years of colonization of the new world.

Perhaps the word that best defines this ancient capital of Lanzarote is "stately". The history of the city's glories and bygone power is written in each and every street, building and monument.

Here are austere convents, beautiful churches, the elegant palaces of the nobility that have kept their seal of distinction and continue to inspire respect in spite of the centuries, and spacious houses in stone

Street market and Santa Bárbara castle.

and brick, with the white walls, large windows and picturesque balconies typical of these the *fortunate isles.*

The visitor to TEGUISE would be well advised to climb up to the top of GUANAPAY to visit the crater of this now extinct volcano and the fortress of SANTA BÁRBARA, constructed in the 15th century, whose keep affords a wonderful view not only of the grey-green countryside of the TEGUISE valley but also of the coast, the sea and the distant dark profile of FUERTEVENTURA and the lesser islands.

This fortress was attacked and destroyed several times, and was finally reconstructed and reinforced by the architect TORRIANI in 1586, since when it has remained unchanged.

An especially interesting visit in SAN MIGUEL DE TEGUISE is the arts and crafts market, where visitors and the inhabitants of the island alike rummage through tiny shops and stalls to discover the most unlikely and fascinating objects produced by the hand of man or by nature.

TEGUISE is also the capital of the "timple", that ancient and most typical of the musical instruments of the CANARY ISLANDS. The secrets of its construction have been passed down from one generation to the next, from father to son. The timple, which is native to the area, is a kind of small guitar whose merry sound, reminiscent of Argentina, faithfully reflects the spirit of the people of the islands, at one and the same time reserved and hospitable.

View of Teguise from Santa Bárbara castle.

Guatiza

GUATIZA is colour, shade, purple; the visitor is inevitably surprised on arriving at GUATIZA to find a village like any other but surrounded by a sea of green, a seemingly endless ocean of cactus whose large, oval protuberances blend into weird geometric forms. Surely only some strange caprice of nature could have brought together in one same place such an enormous quantity of plants that elsewhere grow in defiant solitude. But no, this plantation of spines is the work of man, the plants are as well cared for as a field of wheat.

Cactus and Cochineals.

Entrance to the "Cactus Garden".

"The Cactus Garden".

The explanation is to be found on drawing near to the plants and observing them in detail, for then one can see that they are covered by myriad tiny insects. These are "cochinillas", a strange variety of parasite which, when dead, dried and ground, produces an extraordinary natural tint, cochineal, which is used in cosmetics and dyes for its quality and resistance to external agents. This exotic insect, originally from Mexico, arrived on the island in the 17th century and has since become a permanent inhabitant, contributing significantly to the economy of Lanzarote.

Another outstanding human work is to be found in GUATIZA, the "Jardín de Cactus" or Cactus Garden, created by the great Lanzarote artist CESAR MANRIQUE.

Hundreds of different species of cactus rise from the black ash, creating shapes and perspectives that change as the observer moves along the garden's stone paths, and looming above is the stark whiteness of the windmill of GUATIZA.

Like all the works of Manrique, representative par excellence of the soul of Lanzarote, the cactus garden is an ode to life in the midst of apparent bleakness, a symbol of everything that LANZAROTE has always stood for: the work of man transforming the environment and helping life to triumph over the inanimate.

Jameos del Agua y Cuevas de los Verdes

"La Corona" volcano.

Interior of los Verdes cave.

In the northern part of the island the visitor finds one of those natural phenomena with which LANZAROTE surprises us at every step.

The JAMEOS DEL AGUA is a volcanic tube caused by some ancient eruption of the LA CORONA volcano. This tube cooled and solidified externally, while inside the lava continued to flow. When the flow ran out, the walls collapsed to different depths, giving rise to caves of varying size and length.

One of the most important stretches of these formations is the so-called CUEVA DE LOS VERDES, which measures some two kilometres in length and between 30 and 40 metres in height.

Galleries, passages, natural stairways, labyrinths, underground lagoons flanked by cliffs, seemingly bottomless abysses give the visitor the impression of being the first person to gaze upon these stones and stalactites. But the hand of the artist is present, albeit unseen; a magnificent system of artificial lighting helps nature to show itself in all its splendour, without technology being apparent.

Halls specially prepared for conferences, with a seating capacity for more than five hundred people, or for music, where the stone walls provide sound of outstanding purity; these are just a few of the surprises awaiting the visitor to these natural wonders.

Internal lake in los Jameos del Agua cave.

Entrance to los Verdes cave.

Albino langoustine.

Detail. los Jameos del Agua cave.

Auditorium.

JAMEOS DEL AGUA is the name given to the lower part of the tube, where there is a small underground lake, joined below its surface to the sea. The fauna of this lake has been cut off from the sun for some three thousand years, and includes unique species such as the blind albino langoustine.

The JAMEOS DEL AGUA has been turned into a modern and highly original night club which, without spoiling the natural beauty of the place, provides the visitor with an opportunity to attend musical events in an incomparable setting.

The CUEVA DE LOS VERDES and the JAMEOS DEL AGUA are places privileged by nature where man has acted with sensitivity and love to underline its natural wonders and create unique and fantastic settings.

Los Jameos del Agua swimming pool.

Mirador del Río

Roof skylight in the Mirador bar-restaurant.

On the northern tip of the island is PUNTA FARIONES, an outcrop of rock and lava that cuts like a gigantic knife into the sea. Between this cape and the south-eastern coast of the island "Isla Graciosa" is a passage known as "el río", the river. Some 1,500 feet above the sea, perched atop the PUNTA FARIONES cliff, is the MIRADOR DEL RÍO, an incomparable spot from which to contemplate a view that will not easily be forgotten: the gaze stretches out between sea and sky as if from the prow of some giant ship.

Interior of the Mirador del Río bar-restaurant.

Access passage to the Mirador del Río.

In the most privileged corner of the "mirador" is a peaceful bar-restaurant from whose windows the visitor may gaze out in comfort across a unique view of sky and sea.

In the distance, a horizon of different blues marking the line between sea and air; closer, ISLA GRACIOSA, drawn as if on a map, and the darker outlines of the smaller MONTAÑA CLARA and ALEGRANZA isles; closer still, the thin strip of coast at the foot of a headland that tumbles down to the beach and the sea without a sign of vegetation.

Together, PUNTA FARIONES and EL MIRADOR DEL RÍO are one of the most beautiful and suggestive spots in LANZAROTE and the entire archipelago.

View of "Graciosa" island from the highest part of Mirador del Río.

Famara

Very close to the MIRADOR DEL RÍO is FAMARA, long famous among gastronomy buffs for the excellent fish to be found in the tranquillity of the old fishing village, and no less famous today among fans of para-gliding for the possibilities that its mountains and wide beaches offer for free flight.

Dusk at Famara.

FAMARA is a small fishing port alongside which are ample beaches that stretch along the foot of the PEÑAS DEL CHACHE, magnificent vertical walls from which to launch onto the breeze and descend slowly, and without overmuch risk, in a long flight onto the sand.

Beach, housing development and Graciosa island.

Famara cliffs.

A surfer.

Haría

Haría square.

View of Haría from the Mirador.

HARÍA is a beautiful white village nestling beside the island's most extensive palm grove.

The first thing that catches the visitor's eye is the profusion of flowers of all colours that adorn the balconies and windows of the houses.

HARÍA does not boast any monuments of particular historical or architectural importance, but what is immediately outstanding is the good taste of the town's buildings and the way they blend into the landscape.

The visitor is recommended to visit the museum of popular sacred art, which abounds in wonderful works springing from the imagination of the people of Lanzarote.

Also to be recommended is a short excursion to the MIRADOR DE HARÍA, from where the visitor may contemplate the grandiose spectacle of the CORONA volcano - forger of the JAMEOS DEL AGUA and the CUEVA DE LOS VERDES - and the pastoral landscape of the HARÍA valley, with its oases, palms and white houses.

Constitution square.

Haría palm grove.

Club La Santa

The western coast of the island boasts a particularly beautiful spot that is well worth a visit, LA SANTA. This ancient fishing village now nestles alongside an impressive tourist and sports complex where the visitor may well bump into some of the idols of European sport.

CLUB LA SANTA brings together a wonderful natural landscape of limpid lagoons and top quality sports facilities where the visitor's stay is made pleasant and relaxing by the centre's well distributed installations, tree-lined avenues, gardens and colourful flower beds.

CLUB LA SANTA is a favourite venue among professional footballers, basketball players, athletes, etc. from the north of EUROPE for their pre-season or winter training, both for its top quality sports facilities and for its peaceful, relaxing atmosphere and exceptional climate.

Aerial view of la Santa club.

La Santa club swimming pool.

Facing the development, in the middle of the bay, a small, rounded island emerges from the sea. This is LA ISLETA, an enchanting tropical isle surrounded by an underwater shelf offering excellent fishing, for both anglers and divers. This shelf is relatively shallow and boasts an exceptionally rich marine fauna. Another advantage is that the shelf's absence of currents makes it an ideal place for beginners to dive.

LA SANTA is also outstanding for the excellent conditions it offers for windsurfing, due to its quiet waters and steady breeze, and numerous international competitions and tournaments are organized there throughout the year.

The "small island". (La Isleta).

The club's facilities.

Parque Nacional de Timanfaya

The Timanfaya National Park is one of those natural landscapes of the surprising Canary Island archipelago that would be very difficult to find anywhere else in the world.

This is a natural park in which no endangered plant or animal species are protected; rather it is a mineral museum in full activity: volcanic cones, craters, seas of lava, ash, tongues of liquid magma that spewed from the bowels of the earth to solidify and sculpt natural monuments that defy the imagination, surfaces burnt by fire and temperatures that in certain places reach 400 degrees centigrade just a couple of metres below the ground.

The Devil. the symbol of Timanfaya.

Aerial view.

Camel ride.

Demonstration of underground fire.

Camels returning at dusk.

View of the park from Yaiza.

In this dead area destroyed by fire, life clings on and strives to begin anew: lichens that have adapted to the heat and lack of water have begun to colonize an inhospitable world and to carpet the denuded volcanic rocks, brushing strokes of life and colour on a canvas of black lava.

More than 177 different plant species belonging to 138 genera and 42 families obstinately cling to life and reproduce within the park; fleshy plants spread across the rocks; even more surprisingly, bulrushes grow in rows on the slopes of the volcanic cones, lined up as though planted by the patient hand of a gardener. The presence of these bulrushes is explained by the waterretaining power of volcanic ash and by the fact that the plants take advantage of the moisture carried on the sea breezes.

Animal life is also to be found, represented by insects, reptiles and birds.

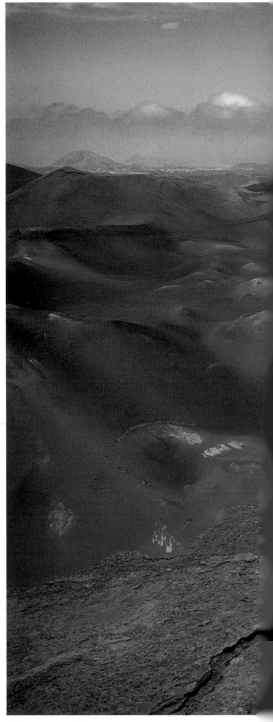

Mountains of Fire.

El Corazoncillo crater.

Restaurant using subteranian volcanic heat to cook.

View of aligned volcanos.

Camels resting.

The TIMANFAYA NATIONAL PARK is a splendid natural laboratory summarizing the history of our planet.

The area which is now the national park is of very remote geological formation, but was shaken in the 17th and 18th centuries by massive eruptions which transformed the most fertile regions of Lanzarote into a desert of death and desolation, burying in their fury entire villages and outlying hamlets and devastating the population and their crops.

Geyser of steam from the earth's core.

A visit to this inhospitable land is a unique, once in a lifetime experience: Montaña de Fuego, Timanfaya, Caldera Bermeja, Los Miraderos, Caldera Rajada, Pedro Perico, Caldera de los Cuervos, Montaña Encantada, Tremesana, Pico Partido, Valle de la Tranquilidad, Barranco del Fuego, Manto de la Virgen,etc..., these are just a few of the names of never to be forgotten places.

Special mention should be made of the ISLOTE DE HILARIO, where there is a restaurant bearing the suggestive name of "EL DIABLO", The Devil, which would have undoubtedly been Jules Verne's favourite. The kitchen at this restaurant, probably the only one of its kind in the world, uses heat coming from the very centre of the earth.

Furnace Mantle del Virgin.

Detail of the park's vegitation.

Panoramic view from Rajada Mountain.

Part view of Timanfaya National Park.

La Geria

At first glance, LA GERIA might appear to a battle field ripped apart by shellfire, but in fact it is not the result of some crazy war but rather the fruit of the inventiveness and the hard and patient work of the peasant farmers of Lanzarote.

LA GERIA is located in an area of volcanic activity, in a landscape of ashes and solidified lava. Over the centuries the area has been razed time and time again by the fury of burning magma, but on each and every occasion its inhabitants have re-

Ingenious protection of the vines.

Wine barrels with the Mountains of Fire as a backdrop.

Aerial view of la Geria.

"Malvasía" wine cellar.

stored its richness and fertility with obstinate tenacity and with the profound knowledge of the soil that man is capable of developing only through love of the land.

In each of these crater-like holes, protected by walls of stone against the winds that blow in from the Atlantic, grow vines that yield abundant crops and produce a wine of outstanding quality: Malvasía, a wine that Shakespeare himself praised highly. "El Grifo" is one of the vineyards that specializes in producing and commercializing the wine that is extracted from the Malvasia grape. In spite of there not being rivers or abundant rains, the holes in which these vines grow capture the humidity swept in by the sea breezes thanks to a fine layer of sand and volcanic ash laid by the farmers, a wonderful example of ecological engineering and popular wisdom.

Yaiza

Anchored in time, the white town of YAIZA has remained unscathed by the changes imposed by fashion.

Although its name is guanche in origin, Yaiza was founded by peasant farmers emigrating from mainland Spain during the early years of colonization of the islands, and this is the way it remains today.

Unlike other towns on the island, Yaiza has not been changed by tourism, although it is no less true that it does not possess the monuments or spectacular scenery of other regions.

Harmonisation of buildings and nature.

Canary Island flower garden.

Hermitage of Nuestra Señora de los Remedios.

Panoramic view of Yaiza.

Well worth a visit is the 16th century hermitage of NUESTRA SEÑORA DE LOS REMEDIOS, reconstructed in the 18th century, whose church houses the image of SAN MARCIAL DEL LIMOGES, patron saint of the island, originally to be found in the cathedral of SAN MARCIAL DEL RUBICÓN in FEMES.

Typical corner.

El Golfo

To the west of YAIZA lies EL GOLFO, a marvellous natural bay still unaffected by tourism or agriculture. This is a veritable paradise waiting to be discovered by visitors in search of peace, tranquillity and savage beauty in all its untouched splendour.

The scenery is just one more of those extraordinary gems that LANZAROTE keeps jealously to itself and then unfolds little by little before the visitor.

Part view of el Golfo.

Aerial view of el Golfo and the fishing village.

Aerial view of the Green Lake. (Charco de los Chicos).

On the beach there is an emerald green lagoon, separated from the sea by a spit of sand and flanked on the other side by a volcanic cliff, stratified into a hypnotic symphony of colours that contrasts with the deep blue of the sea and the brilliant green of the waters at its foot.

EL GOLFO is well worth a visit to enjoy the beauty that nature alone is capable of creating.

Very close to EL GOLFO is a small fishing village which is famous throughout the island for its excellent fresh fish and its cuisine. To be found in the lagoon itself are the strange, semi-precious stones known as "olivinas", with which the local crafts-men make highly original jewellery.

Searching for olivinas.

Los Hervideros

View point of los Hervideros (boiling pots).

The same combination of volcanic eruptions and the relentless attack of the sea that has shaped EL GOLFO has also gone to create an entirely different landscape at LOS HERVIDEROS.

Where in EL GOLFO there is peace and tranquillity at LOS HERVIDEROS there is force and energy; where in the former there are polychromatic cliffs, here is the eternal dark grey of volcanic lava.

This is a cliff-lined coast with enormous boulders tumbling into the sea in a cascade of tangled shapes and deep clefts into which the ocean roars with each surge of the waves. It is this constant surge and roar that gives the place the name of "los hervideros": the boiling pots. Columns of foam shoot upwards into the air, always the same and yet ever changing, embellishing the tortured dark rocks with brilliant arabesques of white lace.

Los Hervideros.

Salinas del Janubio

On the southwestern coast of the island the visitor will encounter a large brackish lake and the salt flats of the SALINAS DEL JANUBIO, an impressive man-made landscape like some immense chequered board of blinding whiteness, surrounded by dark lava and with the deep blue of the sea as a backdrop.

The SALINAS DEL JANUBIO produce most of the salt required by the fishing industry of Lanzarote.

Panoramic view of the Salt Flats of Janubio.

The mounds of salt, lined up in almost military ranks, contrast with the picturesque windmills that dot this area.

The main tourist attractions in the area are "La Hoya" and "Las Breñas", ancient and peaceful villages of stark white, and a wonderful beach of dark volcanic sand.

Panoramic view of the Salt Flats of Janubio.

Playa Blanca

At the southern tip of the island is PLAYA BLANCA, one of LANZAROTE's finest tourist areas.

PLAYA BLANCA, originally a small fishing village, has been transformed in recent years by luxurious residential developments and modern hotels, built to take fullest advantage of the area's benign climate and the quiet transparency of its waters.

The cliffs found in other parts of the island give way here to ample beaches of golden sand. PLAYA BLANCA offers the visitor everything necessary for tranquil but fun-packed holidays in a setting of comfort and quality. First class hotels, developments surrounded by splendid gardens, restaurants and bars where all the languages of the world may be heard, sports complexes, all this is an invitation to the visitor to get away

Promenade and beach of Playa Blanca.

Night view of seafront promenade.

Flamingo Beach.

Seafront promenade.

from the bustle for a few days and spend his time at sports, or just relaxing.

The quiet, limpid waters of Playa Blanca are ideal for exploring in safety the fascinating underwater world, or for indulging in the exciting adventure of skimming across the surface on the wings of the wind.

From PLAYA BLANCA it is an easy matter to sail across to the nearby island of FUERTEVENTURA on one of the ferries that make the crossing daily.

Near to PLAYA BLANCA, at PUNTA PECHIGUERAS, is the island's only lighthouse.

PAPAGAYO is the name given to a string of golden beaches and sandy coves among the coastal cliffs between "Playa Blanca" and "Punta del Papagayo". Clear, calm waters and quiet, solitary coves, a world removed from time and without any sense of rush, ideal for fishing, swimming, diving, sunbathing or simply enjoying the pleasure to be derived from doing nothing.

Golden Sand Beach.

Boat ferry to Fuerteventura.

On one of these beaches stands the castle of LAS COLORADAS, constructed in the 18th century, which closed the island's defence system to the south. Destroyed on several occasions and then rebuilt, the castle has recently been restored once more.

PAPAGAYO is a world of peace and restfulness, of smooth beaches and quiet waters in which to get away from things and discover the pleasure of contemplation.

Las Coloradas castle.

Flamingo Beach.

Papagayo beaches.

Papagayo beaches.

Puerto del Carmen

If ARRECIFE is the administrative and commercial centre of LANZAROTE and SAN MIGUEL DE TEGUISE the island's historical capital, PUERTO DEL CARMEN is undoubtedly its tourist Mecca.

From ARRECIFE southwards are twenty kilometres of low-lying coast with the island's most beautiful and inviting beaches.

PUERTO DEL CARMEN is the most important centre in this area, and offers the visitor comfortable hotels, sports facilities, nightlife and major shopping centres.

PUERTO DEL CARMEN is flanked on either side by the beautiful, easily accessed beaches of "Playa Grande" and "Playa Quemada", with elegant, wooded residential areas that stretch along the sea front.

Just to the north of PUERTO DEL CARMEN is LANZAROTE's only airport, capable of handling both transoceanic flights and the domestic traffic linking the island to the others in the Canary archipelago and to mainland Spain.

The airport is modern, comfortable and hospitable, and reflects the style

Sunset over the seafront promenade.

Grande beach.

Puerto del Carmen dry dock.

Pila de la Barrilla beach.

Palm trees, sea and sand.

Dusk over Puerto del Carmen.

Grande beach.

Chica beach.

Puerto del Carmen dry dock.

of Lanzarote's great artist CESAR MAN-RIQUE, who participated actively in its design and decoration.

In spite of the fact that most of the tourists visiting Lanzarote prefer to stay in the area around PUERTO DEL CARMEN, the town's open spaces and the careful design and distribution of its hotels, residential developments, sports and recreational facilities and shopping areas allow visitors to enjoy their holiday in comfort, without the crowds so typical of many other tourist centres, even of those costing a lot more.

Los Pocillos beach.

Nightfall at los Pocillos.

Matagorda seafront promenade.

The villages of "Los Pocitos" and "Matagorda" have now joined Puerto del Carmen in offering hotel accommodation along this part of the coast.

Their beaches join those described above in offering the visitor space to enjoy the wonderful waters of Lanzarote's Atlantic coast.

Windsurfing.

Blanca beach.

Panoramic view of Grande beach.

Puerto del Carmen dry dock.

La Peñita beaches.

Los Fariones hotel beach.

Fundación César Manrique

The Cesar Manrique Foundation was born with a vocation, to become an open, receptive cultural centre at the service of the local community. The philosophy of the centre is one of active participation in the cultural alternatives and proposals offered by the Islands and by the State itself, with special attention given to the plastic arts, and of creating an artistic space within the formula ART-NATURE/NATURE-ART.

The Foundation is located in Taro de Tahíche, a village belonging to the municipal area of Teguise, the ancient capital of Lanzarote. A large part of the 30,000 m2 plot on which the house is built is occupied by an impressive

César Manrique.

tongue of lava from the eruption that occurred in 1730-36.

To the intrinsic and evident artistic characteristics of this surprising edifice - built in 1968 and until 1987 the home of the artist - is added the symbolic value attributed to it on the island and elsewhere as an exemplary and pioneer way of using an amazing natural formation: five volcanic bubbles set in a sea of lava.

The upper part of the outside of the house is clearly inspired by the traditional architecture of Lanzarote, while the lower, underground level, which is volcanic in nature, is spectacular in the way it is built around and conserves the volcanic bubbles described above.

The César Manrique Foundation.

Entrance to the Foundation.

The Foundation has two collections of contemporary art, donated by César Manrique One of these, the "Colección Manrique", is made up of paintings, sculptures, drawings, sketches and other objects by the painter himself. The other, the "Colección particular", which was previously Manrique's own private collection, includes the works of other artists, among them Picasso, Miró, Tápies, Soto, Le Parc, Equipo Crónica, Fraile, Mompo, Guerrero, Manolo Millares, Sempere, Martín Chirino, Gerardo Rueda, Pedro González, Gerardo Delgado, Cardenas, Cuixart, Zóbel,...

Exterior mural.